Washington Commanders Trivia Quiz Book

500 Questions on all things Burgundy and Gold

Chris Bradshaw

All rights reserved. Copyright © 2022 Chris Bradshaw. All rights reserved. No portion of this book may be reproduced in any form without permission from the publisher, except as permitted by U.S. copyright law.

Every effort has been made by the author and publishing house to ensure that the information contained in this book was correct as of press time. The author and publishing house hereby disclaim and do not assume liability for any injury, loss, damage, or disruption caused by errors or omissions, regardless of whether any errors or omissions result from negligence, accident, or any other cause. Readers are encouraged to verify any information contained in this book prior to taking any action on the information.

For rights and permissions, please contact:

C_D_Bradshaw@hotmail.com

ISBN: 1-7396883-9-4
ISBN-13: 978-1-7396883-9-4

Front cover image created by headfuzz by grimboid. Check out his great selection of sport, movie, music and TV posters online at:

https://www.etsy.com/shop/headfuzzbygrimboid

Introduction

Think you know about the Washington Commanders? Put your knowledge to the test with this collection of quizzes on all things burgundy and gold.

The book covers the whole history of the Washington franchise, including the glorious Joe Gibbs Super Bowl era right through to the recent revival under Ron Rivera.

The biggest names in team history are present and correct so look out for questions on Joe Theismann, Antonio Gibson, Darrell Green, Dexter Manley, John Riggins, Art Monk, Terry McLaurin and many, many more.

There are 500 questions in all covering running backs and receivers, coaches and quarterbacks, pass rushers and punters and much else besides.

Each quiz contains a selection of 20 questions and is either a mixed bag of pot luck testers or is centered on a specific category such as the 1990s or defense.

There are easy, medium and hard questions offering something for Commanders rookies as well as seasoned Washington watchers.

You'll find the answers to each quiz below the bottom of the following quiz. For example, the answers to Quiz 1: Super Bowl Champions, are underneath Quiz 2: Pot Luck. The only exception is Quiz 25: Anagrams. The answers to these can be found under the Quiz 1 questions.

All statistics relate to the regular season only unless otherwise stated and are accurate to the start of the 2022 season.

We hope you enjoy the Washington Commanders Trivia Quiz Book.

About the Author

Chris Bradshaw has written more than 30 quiz books including titles for Britain's biggest selling daily newspaper, The Sun, and The Times (of London). In addition to the NFL, he has written extensively on soccer, cricket, darts and poker.

He lives in Birmingham, England and has been following the NFL for over 30 years.

Acknowledgements

Many thanks to Ken and Veronica Bradshaw, Heidi Grant, Steph, James, Ben and Will Roe, Garry Maddocks and Graham Nash.

CONTENTS

1	Super Bowl Champions	8
2	Pot Luck	10
3	Running Backs	12
4	Pot Luck	14
5	Receivers	16
6	Pot Luck	18
7	Quarterbacks	20
8	Pot Luck	22
9	Defense	24
10	Pot Luck	26
11	Special Teams	28
12	Pot Luck	30
13	1970s	32
14	Pot Luck	34
15	1980s	36
16	Pot Luck	38
17	1990s	40

18	Pot Luck	42
19	2000s	44
20	Pot Luck	46
21	2010 and Beyond	48
22	Pot Luck	50
23	Numbers Game	52
24	Pot Luck	54
25	Anagrams	56

Quiz 1: Super Bowl Champions

1. Which coach steered Washington to their three Super Bowl victories?

2. Which team did Washington face in Super Bowl XVII?

3. What was the final score of Super Bowl XVII?

4. True or false – The Washington defense allowed just four pass completions in Super Bowl XVII?

5. Super Bowl XVII was hosted in which stadium?

6. Who was named the game's Most Valuable Player?

7. Which team did the 1987 Washington team face in Super Bowl XXII?

8. What was the final score in the game?

9. How many unanswered points did Washington score in the second quarter of Super Bowl XXII?

10. Super Bowl XXII was hosted in which city?

11. Who was the MVP of Super Bowl XXII?

12. Which legendary rock and roll star performed the half-time show at Super Bowl XXII?

13. Which running back rushed for 204 yards from 22 carries in Super Bowl XXII?

14. What was the name of the Washington kicker who booted six extra points in Super Bowl XXII?

15. Washington made it a hat-trick of World Championships after defeating which team in Super Bowl XXVI?

16. What was the final score in Super Bowl XXVI?

17. Which stadium hosted Super Bowl XXVI?

18. Who was named the game's MVP?

19. Which two Washington players caught touchdown passes in Super Bowl XXVI?

20. Which crooner sang the national anthem prior to Super Bowl XXVI?

Quiz 25: Answers

1. Joe Gibbs 2. Art Monk 3. Kirk Cousins 4. Ryan Kerrigan 5. John Riggins 6. Darrell Green 7. Clinton Portis 8. Dexter Manley 9. Santana Moss 10. London Fletcher 11. Jordan Reed 12. Mark Moseley 13. Joe Theismann 14. Doug Williams 15. Antonio Gibson 16. Trent Williams 17. Mark Rypien 18. Alfred Morris 19. Charles Mann 20. Terry McLaurin

Quiz 2: Pot Luck

1. Which former Washington general manager was inducted into the Pro Football Hall of Fame as part of the Class of 2018?

2. What three-word phrase went viral after Kirk Cousins engineered an epic 2015 comeback against the Bucs?

3. Who was the last Washington player to win the AP NFL Rookie of the Year Award?

4. Since 1982, who are the three Washington players with over 80 sacks?

5. Which defensive lineman became the NFL's all-time leader in sacks during his brief stay with Washington?

6. Who is the current owner of Washington franchise?

7. Who holds the record for the most yards from scrimmage in franchise history?

8. True or false – Washington wore white jerseys in all three of their Super Bowl triumphs?

9. Who was the first Washington quarterback to average over 300 yards per game in a season?

10. Who holds the franchise record for the most receptions in a season by a tight end?

11. Which linebacker did Washington select with the second overall pick of the 2000 NFL Draft?

12. Who was named the AP NFL Defensive Rookie of the Year for 2020?

13. Which offensive lineman turned broadcaster won a Super Bowl ring with Washington then two more with the Broncos?

14. Which quarterback holds the record for the most 300-yard passing games in franchise history?

15. Washington defeated which division rival in 1975 to claim their first ever overtime win?

16. Who caught a 68-yard touchdown pass from Mark Brunell to give Washington a 36-30 overtime win over the Jags in October 2006?

17. Which full back tied a team record after scoring three rushing touchdowns in a 2013 overtime win over the Chargers?

18. Which former Washington player appears on Twitter under the username @J_No24?

19. What is former defensive lineman Ziggy Hood's real first name? a) Evander b) Lennox c) Tyson

20. How many seasons did Darrell Green spend with Washington? a) 18 b) 19 c) 20

Quiz 1: Answers

1. Joe Gibbs 2. Miami 3. Washington 27-17 Miami 4. True 5. The Rose Bowl 6. John Riggins 7. Denver 8. Washington 42-10 Denver 9. 35 10. San Diego 11. Doug Williams 12. Chubby Checker 13. Timmy Smith 14. Ali Haji Sheikh 15. Buffalo 16. Washington 37-21 Buffalo 17. Metrodome 18. Mark Rypien 19. Earnest Byner and Gary Clark 20. Harry Connick Jr.

Quiz 3: Running Backs

1. With 7,242 yards who is Washington's all-time leading rusher?

2. Who rushed for over 1,000 yards in 2012, 2013 and 2014?

3. Who rushed for hat-trick of touchdowns in Washington's 2020 Thanksgiving Day win over the Cowboys?

4. Who rushed a franchise record 45 times in a 1988 game against the Bengals?

5. Who holds the record for the most rushing touchdowns in franchise history?

6. 'Fat Rob' was the nickname of which former Washington running back?

7. Which Heisman Trophy winner rushed for 206 yards against the Cardinals in December 1985?

8. Who holds the franchise record for the most rushing yards in a single season?

9. Who rushed for over 1,000 yards in three successive seasons from 1999 to 2001?

10. Of Washington backs with over 750 rushes, who has the best yards per carry average?

11. Who are the two Washington backs to have led the team in season rushing touchdowns five times?

12. Which back scored 21 rushing touchdowns during the 1996 season?

13. Who are the two Washington backs to rush for over 1,000 yards in their rookie season?

14. True or false – Washington hasn't used a first-round draft pick on a running back since the 1960s?

15. Which rusher enjoyed back-to-back 1,000-yard seasons in 1990 and 1991?

16. Whose 85-yard run against the Eagles in September 1993 is the second longest in franchise history?

17. Who was the last Washington player to lead the NFL in rushing yards?

18. Who rushed for a franchise record 221 yards against the Eagles in September 1989?

19. Who holds the franchise record for the most career 100-yard games? a) Alfred Morris b) Clinton Portis c) John Riggins

20. How many rushing touchdowns did John Riggins score in 1983? a) 22 b) 23 c) 24

Quiz 2: Answers

1. Bobby Beathard 2. "You like that" 3. Robert Griffin III 4. Dexter Manley, Charles Mann and Ryan Kerrigan 5. Bruce Smith 6. Daniel Snyder 7. Art Monk 8. True 9. Kirk Cousins 10. Jordan Reed 11. LaVar Arrington 12. Chase Young 13. Mark Schlereth 14. Kirk Cousins 15. Dallas 16. Santana Moss 17. Darrel Young 18. Josh Norman 19. a) Evander 20. c) 20

Quiz 4: Pot Luck

1. Which quarterback is the only Washington player to wear the #7 jersey in franchise history?

2. What number jersey did pass rusher Ryan Kerrigan wear?

3. Who are the two Washington backs to rush for a touchdown in 13 successive games?

4. Who was the last offensive tackle selected by Washington in the first round of the NFL Draft?

5. Who holds the record for the most career appearances for Washington?

6. Which tight end went to the Pro Bowl for the first time in 2016?

7. Washington acquired Clinton Portis from which team?

8. Which defensive back moved in the opposite direction as part of the Portis deal?

9. Which Washington guard was named on the NFL's 1980s All-Decade First Team?

10. Who holds the franchise record for the most yards from scrimmage in a single season?

11. Who was appointed Washington's offensive coordinator prior to the start of the 2021 season?

12. Which future NFL head coach was the offensive coordinator on Washington's 1982 World Championship team?

13. Jordan Reed holds the NFL record for the fewest number of games to reach 200 catches by a tight end. Which Hall of Famer was the previous holder of that record?

14. True or false – In 2001, Washington became the first team to lose their first five games then win the five games that followed?

15. Which quarterback, making his first start with the team, led Washington to a 20-17 overtime win over Dallas in October 2014?

16. 2022 first-round draft pick Jahan Dotson played college ball at which school?

17. What number jersey did star defensive back Darrell Green wear?

18. Which Hall of Fame defensive lineman ended his career in Washington, kicking an extra point in his final appearance in 1974?

19. What is the highest attendance for a game at FedEx Field? a) 88,910 b) 89,910 c) 90,910

20. In December 2018, Washington registered the 600th win in franchise history after beating which opponent? a) Indianapolis b) Jacksonville c) Tennessee

Quiz 3: Answers

1. John Riggins 2. Alfred Morris 3. Antonio Gibson 4. Jamie Morris 5. John Riggins 6. Robert Kelley 7. George Rogers 8. Alfred Morris 9. Stephen Davis 10. Alfred Morris 11. Clinton Portis and John Riggins 12. Terry Allen 13. Alfred Morris and Reggie Brooks 14. True 15. Earnest Byner 16. Reggie Brooks 17. Larry Brown 18. Gerald Riggs 19. b) Clinton Portis 20. c) 24

Quiz 5: Receivers

1. With 12,026 yards, who is Washington's all-time leading receiver?

2. In 2005, who set the record for the most receiving yards in a single season with 1,483?

3. Whose 113 catches in 2013 are the most by a Washington receiver in a single season?

4. In 2015, who became the first tight end since the 1970s to lead the team in receiving yards?

5. Which tight end caught 429 passes in a career that stretched from 2004 to 2012?

6. In 1984, who became the first Washington receiver to catch over 100 passes in a single season?

7. Which receiver caught a 52-yard bomb from Kirk Cousins against the Raiders in September 2017 to score his first NFL touchdown?

8. Which receiver led the team in touchdown catches in six out of seven seasons between 1986 and 1992?

9. Who caught 9 passes for 193 yards and two touchdowns in the Super Bowl XXII rout of Denver?

10. Which receiver caught touchdown passes in six straight games (including the playoffs) in 2007?

11. In 2019, who became the first player in NFL history to register at least five catches and score a touchdown in each of his first three career games?

12. Since 1970, of players with over 200 receptions for Washington, who has the highest yards per catch average?

13. Which receiver holds the record for catching the most touchdown passes in franchise history?

14. Which former Texan, Patriot and Bronco led the team in receptions and yards in 2011, his only season with Washington?

15. Which receiver's six games of 100 yards or more in 2014 is tied for second-most in a season in franchise history?

16. Art Monk is one of two Washington receivers with five 1,000-yard receiving seasons. Who is the other?

17. Who is the only Washington player to have led the NFL in catches in a season more than once?

18. Who set the franchise record for the most catches by a rookie after grabbing 59 passes in 2015?

19. How many regular season-catches did Art Monk make in his career? a) 666 b) 777 c) 888

20. Between 1983 and 1993 Art Monk caught passes in how many consecutive games? a) 144 b) 154 c) 164

Quiz 4: Answers

1. Joe Theismann 2. #91 3. John Riggins and George Rogers 4. Trent Williams 5. Darrell Green 6. Jordan Reed 7. Denver 8. Champ Bailey 9. Russ Grimm 10. Clinton Portis 11. Scott Turner 12. Joe Bugel 13. Kellen Winslow 14. True 15. Colt McCoy 16. Penn State 17. #28 18. Deacon Jones 19. c) 90,910 20. b) Jacksonville

Quiz 6: Pot Luck

1. In which decade was the franchise founded?

2. Prior to Chase Young in 2020, who was the last Washington rookie defender voted to the Pro Bowl?

3. Who had more 100-yard receiving games with Washington – Gary Clark or Ricky Sanders?

4. Which tight end played for Washington in the 1970s, 1980s and 1990s?

5. Head coach Ron Rivera won a Super Bowl ring as a player with which team?

6. Whose #33 jersey is the only number to be officially retired by Washington?

7. Who was the first Washington back to rush for over 1,000 yards in three successive seasons?

8. True or false – Washington great Charles Mann launched a range of sausages called 'Man Oh Mann'?

9. Who are the three Washington quarterbacks since 1970 to have thrown for over 25 touchdowns in a single season?

10. Prior to Ron Rivera in 2020, who was the last Washington head coach to steer the team to the playoffs in his first season in charge?

11. In 1988, Washington used their first selection in the NFL Draft (in round two) to select which kicker?

12. Former quarterback Robert Griffin III was born in which Asian country?

13. Which Hall of Fame cornerback spent a single season with Washington in 2000?

14. Head coach Joe Gibbs recorded his 150th career win in 2005 in a 52-17 rout of which team?

15. True or false – Washington was the first franchise in NFL history to record 600 wins?

16. Defensive lineman Jonathan Allen played college ball at which school?

17. Prior to Tress Way in 2019, who was the last Washington punter voted to the Pro Bowl?

18. Who holds the franchise record for the most 100-yard receiving games?

19. Up to the start of the 2022 season, Washington had won how many regular season games in their history? a) 607 b) 617 c) 627

20. What was the nickname of star running back John Riggins? a) Diesel b) Oil c) Petrol

Quiz 5: Answers

1. Art Monk 2. Santana Moss 3. Pierre Garcon 4. Jordan Reed 5. Chris Cooley 6. Art Monk 7. Josh Doctson 8. Gary Clark 9. Ricky Sanders 10. Santana Moss 11. Terry McLaurin 12. Henry Ellard 13. Charley Taylor 14. Jabar Gaffney 15. DeSean Jackson 16. Gary Clark 17. Charley Taylor 18. Jamison Crowder 19. c) 888 20. c) 164

Quiz 7: Quarterbacks

1. Who holds the record for the most passing yards in franchise history?

2. Washington drafted Kirk Cousins from which college?

3. Which former Washington quarterback was named the team's Senior Vice President of Player Personnel in 2017?

4. Who are the two Washington quarterbacks in the Pro Football Hall of Fame?

5. Who holds the franchise record for the most pass attempts in a single season with 606?

6. Who is the only Washington quarterback to throw four touchdown passes in a single postseason game?

7. In which round of the 2012 NFL Draft did Washington select Kirk Cousins?

8. Who has the most 400-yard passing games in franchise history?

9. Which Super Bowl-winning quarterback spent an early part of his career in the Canadian Football League with the Toronto Argonauts?

10. Who holds the franchise record for most passing yards in a game after throwing for 471 yards against the Bucs in 1999?

11. Since 1990, Washington has used a first-round draft pick to select a quarterback five times. Name the quintet.

12. Who tied an unwanted franchise record in December 1986 after throwing six interceptions against the Giants?

20

13. Who holds the franchise record for the most career touchdown passes thrown in the playoffs?

14. Of quarterbacks with over 1,000 attempts, who has the lowest interception percentage?

15. Who threw more touchdown passes with Washington – Kirk Cousins or Mark Rypien?

16. Who tied a franchise record after throwing six touchdown passes in a 1991 game against Atlanta?

17. Which quarterback has been sacked the most times in franchise history?

18. Who holds the franchise record for throwing the most passes in a game without an interception?

19. Who holds the record for the most touchdown passes in a season? a) Sonny Jurgensen b) Mark Rypien c) Joe Theismann

20. How many touchdown passes were thrown to set that single-season record? a) 31 b) 32 c) 33

Quiz 6: Answers

1. 1930s 2. Brian Orakpo 3. Gary Clark 4. Don Warren 5. Chicago Bears 6. Sammy Baugh 7. Stephen Davis 8. True 9. Joe Theismann, Kirk Cousins and Mark Rypien 10. George Allen 11. Chip Lohmiller 12. Japan 13. Deion Sanders 14. San Francisco 15. False 16. Alabama 17. Matt Turk 18. Art Monk 19. b) 617 games 20. a) Diesel

Quiz 8: Pot Luck

1. What number jersey did star running back John Riggins wear?

2. Who had more 100-yard receiving games with Washington – Santana Moss or DeSean Jackson?

3. Who was named the NFL's Comeback Player of the Year for 2020?

4. Who is the only Washington quarterback to throw 20 touchdown passes in his rookie season?

5. Which Washington player was the first African-American starting quarterback to win a Super Bowl?

6. In the 1990s, Washington twice used their first-round draft pick to select a wide receiver. Can you name the pair?

7. Who holds the record for the most combined yards (including kick returns) in Washington's history?

8. Who returned an Eli Manning interception for a touchdown in his NFL debut against the Giants in 2011?

9. Before Carson Wentz, who was the last quarterback to start a season opener with three different teams in three straight seasons?

10. After retiring from Washington in 1992, coach Joe Gibbs turned his attention to which sport?

11. In a September 2022 game against Dallas the Commanders wore what color uniforms for the first time?

12. Who caught four passes for a massive 208 yards in a 1991 game against Atlanta?

13. In 2016, Washington recorded their first tied game since 1997 against which team?

14. True or false – At least one Washington player has been selected to the Pro Bowl every year since its inception?

15. In 2002, Washington played an exhibition game in which Asian country?

16. Who holds the franchise record for the most 100-yard rushing games in a single season?

17. How many times did he break the century mark that season?

18. Which of Washington's Super Bowl-winning quarterbacks was born in Canada?

19. Washington secured the 2020 NFC East title by defeating which team 20-14 in the season finale? a) Dallas b) NY Giants c) Philadelphia

20. What was the nickname of tight end Don Warren? a) The Dane b) The Dutchman c) The German

Quiz 7: Answers

1. Joe Theismann 2. Michigan State 3. Doug Williams 4. Sammy Baugh and Sonny Jurgensen 5. Kirk Cousins 6. Doug Williams 7. Fourth 8. Kirk Cousins 9. Joe Theismann 10. Brad Johnson 11. Heath Shuler, Patrick Ramsey, Jason Campbell, Robert Griffin III and Dwayne Haskins 12. Jay Schroeder 13. Joe Theismann 14. Robert Griffin III 15. Mark Rypien 16. Mark Rypien 17. Joe Thiesmann 18. Alex Smith 19. a) Sonny Jurgensen 20. c) 33

Quiz 9: Defense

1. Who holds the franchise record for the most sacks in a single season with 18.5?

2. Which star defensive tackle did Washington select with their first pick in the 2017 NFL Draft?

3. Which Hall of Fame defender recorded 29 sacks in a spell in Washington that lasted from 2000 until 2003?

4. Who holds the franchise record for the most career interceptions?

5. With which pick of the 2020 NFL Draft did Washington select Chase Young?

6. Which defensive back picked off two John Elway passes in Super Bowl XXII?

7. Which linebacker was named an All-Pro four times and went to nine Pro Bowls between 1966 and 1976?

8. Which multiple Pro Bowl defensive end was nicknamed 'C-Ment'?

9. True or false – Dexter Manley never went to the Pro Bowl?

10. Which Washington linebacker went to the Pro Bowl every year from 2009 through to 2012?

11. Which former Chicago linebacker recorded a game-high 11 tackles, one sack and two forced fumbles in Super Bowl XXVI?

12. Which Washington defensive back led the NFL in interceptions in 1987?

13. In 2009, which linebacker became the first Washington rookie to make the Pro Bowl in over 30 years?

14. Who led the team in interceptions in 2009, 2010 and 2011?

15. Which linebacker appeared in 215 games for Washington between 1979 and 1994?

16. In 2014, Washington set a franchise record by recording 10 sacks in a game against which AFC team?

17. Who is the all-time leading tackler in Washington's history?

18. Which dominant Washington defender was nicknamed 'Secretary of Defense'?

19. Which opponent has thrown for the most passing yards against the Washington defense in franchise history? a) Troy Aikman b) Eli Manning c) Tony Romo

20. What is the most sacks that the Washington defense has recorded in a single season? a) 64 b) 66 c) 68

Quiz 8: Answers

1. #44 2. Santana Moss 3. Alex Smith 4. Robert Griffin III 5. Doug Williams 6. Michael Westbrook and Desmond Howard 7. Brian Mitchell 8. Ryan Kerrigan 9. Donovan McNabb 10. NASCAR 11. Black 12. Gary Clark 13. Cincinnati 14. False 15. Japan 16. Clinton Portis 17. 9 times 18. Mark Rypien 19. a) Philadelphia 20. b) The Dutchman

Quiz 10: Pot Luck

1. 'Slinging Sammy' was the nickname of which legendary Washington quarterback?

2. Who was the last left-handed starting quarterback to win a game for Washington?

3. Who holds the record for the most sacks by a Washington player in the playoffs with 10 between 1983 and 1992?

4. What does the J in the name of running back J.D. McKissic stand for?

5. Which defensive back has brothers called Kyle, Vincent and Corey, all of whom have played in the NFL?

6. Which former Washington great wrote the book 'The Complete Idiot's Guide to Understanding Football Like a Pro'?

7. True or false – In the 16 seasons in which Joe Gibbs was head coach, Washington never wore burgundy jerseys in a home game?

8. You have to go back to 1991 to find the last Washington player to lead the NFL in scoring. Which kicker managed that feat?

9. True of false – Tight end Vernon Davis was an honorary captain of the US curling team at the 2010 Winter Olympics?

10. Quarterback Carson Wentz was drafted by which team with the second overall pick of the 2016 NFL Draft?

11. Who are the two Washington quarterbacks to throw for over 300 yards in three successive games?

12. Who are the four Washington quarterbacks to have started all 16 regular season games in back-to-back seasons?

13. Prior to Terry McLaurin in 2020 and 2021 who was the last Washington receiver with back-to-back 1,000-yard seasons?

14. Legendary quarterback Sonny Jurgensen was originally drafted by which divisional rival?

15. Who caught seven passes for a franchise record 255 yards and three touchdowns against the Rams in October 1987?

16. True or false – In the early sixties Washington endured a barren run of 21 games without a win?

17. Darrell Green picked off at least one pass in how many successive seasons?

18. Which Hall of Fame receiver, best known for his time with the Bills, ended his career with Washington in 2000?

19. What is the highest number of turnovers created by Washington in a single season? a) 41 b) 51 c) 61

20. How long is the longest pass in franchise history? a) 97 yards b) 98 yards c) 99 yards

Quiz 9: Answers

1. Dexter Manley 2. Jonathan Allen 3. Bruce Smith 4. Darrell Green 5. Second 6. Barry Wilburn 7. Chris Hanburger 8. Charles Mann 9. False 10. London Fletcher 11. Wilber Marshall 12. Barry Wilburn 13. Brian Orakpo 14. DeAngelo Hall 15. Monte Coleman 16. Jacksonville 17. Darrell Green 18. Dexter Manley 19. b) Eli Manning 20. c) 66

Quiz 11: Special Teams

1. Who is Washington's all-time leading points scorer?

2. Dustin Hopkins tied a franchise record after going five for five on field goals in a 2016 game against which division rival?

3. What is the longest successful field goal in franchise history?

4. Who converted that record-breaking kick against the Giants in November 2011?

5. Whose 896 punts between 1968 and 1979 are the most in franchise history?

6. Which explosive Washington returner went to the Pro Bowl in 1980, 1981 and 1982?

7. Who led the team in punt returns for nine successive seasons between 1991 and 1999?

8. Who are the two Washington kickers to lead the NFL in scoring in successive seasons?

9. Who returned a kickoff for a 100-yard touchdown in an October 2021 game against Atlanta?

10. Who tied a franchise record after returning a kickoff 101-yards for a touchdown against the Giants in September 2015?

11. Which Washington long snapper played half of the 2012 win over New Orleans despite suffering from a broken arm?

12. Which alliteratively named punter tied a franchise record in 2004 after punting 103 times?

13. Who returned a punt 85 yards for a touchdown against the Ravens in October 2016?

14. Which kicker converted 18 straight field goals during the closing stages of the 2013 and start of the 2014 seasons?

15. Who holds the franchise record for converting the most field goals in a single season?

16. Who tied a franchise record in 2011 after converting four field goals of 50 yards or longer?

17. The award given to Washington's special teams player of the year is named after which former player?

18. Which punter went to the Pro Bowl in 1996, 1997 and 1998?

19. Between 1988 and 1990 Chip Lohmiller kicked a field goal in how many consecutive games? a) 27 b) 28 c) 29

20. Mark Moseley successfully converted how many straight fields goals in 1981 and 1982? a) 19 b) 21 c) 23

Quiz 10: Answers

1. Sammy Baugh 2. Mark Brunell 3. Charles Mann 4. Joshua 5. Kendall Fuller 6. Joe Theismann 7. True 8. Chip Lohmiller 9. True 10. Philadelphia 11. Kirk Cousins and Robert Griffin III 12. Theismann, Cousins, Rypien and Campbell 13. Henry Ellard 14. Philadelphia 15. Anthony Allen 16. True 17. 19 seasons 18. Andre Reed 19. c) 61 20. c) 99 yards

Quiz 12: Pot Luck

1. Who were the two Washington QBs to throw touchdown passes during the 2021 season?

2. Which former Washington offensive star was a finalist for the 2008 Joe Montana High School Quarterback of the Year Award?

3. What number jersey does Terry McLaurin wear?

4. 'Bosco' was the nickname of which long-serving Washington center?

5. @DaHop5 is the Twitter handle of which long-time Washington player?

6. Which quarterback fumbled a franchise-record five times during a 2002 game against Green Bay?

7. Which team defeated Washington 73-0 in the 1940 NFL Championship decider?

8. The Commanders acquired Carson Wentz following a trade with which team?

9. True or false – Star running back John Riggins sat out the whole of the 1980 season due to a contract dispute?

10. Who was the only defensive player from Washington to be selected to the 2021 NFC Pro Bowl roster?

11. Of Washington quarterbacks with over 1,500 passes, who has the highest completion percentage?

12. Who was the only offensive player from Washington to be selected to the 2021 NFC Pro Bowl roster?

13. Who set an NFL record after catching at least five passes in 19 successive games in 2002 and 2003?

14. Which quarterback appeared for his ninth different NFL team during an injury shortened stint in Washington in 2021?

15. Who had more 300-yard passing games with Washington – Mark Brunell or Jay Schroeder?

16. Which quarterback tied for the team lead in rushing touchdowns in 2011 despite scoring just two of them?

17. What number jersey did wide receiver Santana Moss wear?

18. True or false – Up to the start of the 2022 season, Washington had beaten the Kansas City Chiefs only once in franchise history?

19. Up to the close of the 2021 season, Washington had appeared in how many playoff games? a) 37 b) 40 c) 43

20. What is the fewest number of turnovers created by Washington in a single season? a) 12 b) 13 c) 14

Quiz 11: Answers

1. Mark Moseley 2. New York Giants 3. 59 yards 4. Graham Gano 5. Mike Bragg 6. Mike Nelms 7. Brian Mitchell 8. Mark Moseley and Chip Lohmiller 9. DeAndre Carter 10. Rashad Ross 11. Nick Sundberg 12. Tom Tupa 13. Jamison Crowder 14. Kai Forbath 15. Dustin Hopkins 16. Graham Gano 17. Mark Moseley 18. Matt Turk 19. b) 28 games 20. c) 23

Quiz 13: 1970s

1. Who was Washington coach from 1971 through to 1977?

2. Which team did Washington face in Super Bowl VII?

3. What was the score in that game?

4. Which quarterback led Washington to Super Bowl VII?

5. Which team did Washington defeat in the 1972 NFC Championship Game?

6. Which defensive back scored Washington's only touchdown in Super Bowl VII?

7. Who were the three Washington players to lead the team in rushing in the 1970s?

8. True or false – No Washington receiver enjoyed a 1,000-yard season during the 1970s?

9. Which team eliminated Washington in the divisional round of the playoffs in 1973 and 1976?

10. Which Washington linebacker was named a first-team All-Pro in 1972, 1973 and 1975?

11. Which wide receiver became the NFL's all-time leader in receptions in 1975 after grabbing his 634th pass?

12. In 1973, which running back set the franchise record for the most yards from scrimmage in a single game with 255?

13. Which tight end led the team in touchdown catches in 1976, 1977 and 1978?

14. Which former player was appointed the team's 19th head coach in 1978?

15. Which Washington quarterback recorded the most regular season wins with the team in the 1970s?

16. Which defensive back, whose surname is the same as a major US city, led the team in interceptions in 1973, 1975 and 1977?

17. Which former Cincinnati Bengal was named an All-Pro in 1979 after picking off nine passes?

18. Which quarterback, who started two games in 1975, shares his name with an all-time great baseball pitcher?

19. What was the most regular season wins recorded by Washington in a single season during the 1970s? a) 9 b) 10 c) 11

20. What was the highest number of losses Washington suffered in a single season during the 1970s? a) 8 b) 9 c) 10

Quiz 12: Answers

1. Taylor Heinicke and Kyle Allen 2. Jordan Reed 3. #17 4. Jeff Bostic 5. Dustin Hopkins 6. Patrick Ramsey 7. Chicago Bears 8. Indianapolis 9. True 10. Jonathan Allen 11. Kirk Cousins 12. Brandon Scherff 13. Laveranues Coles 14. Ryan Fitzpatrick 15. Jay Schroeder 16. John Beck 17. #89 18. True 19. c) 43 20. a) 12

Quiz 14: Pot Luck

1. Do Washington have an overall winning or losing record against the Eagles?

2. In 1994, who became the first Washington player to lead the NFC in sacks?

3. Whom did Jay Gruden succeed as Washington head coach?

4. Which offensive lineman holds the franchise record for the most playoff games played with 21?

5. Who is the play-by-play announcer on Commanders radio broadcasts?

6. True or false – Washington is unbeaten in home NFC Championship games?

7. Which coach, who took his team to multiple Super Bowls in the 1990s, was Washington's special teams coach in the early 1970s?

8. Prior to Jonathan Allen, who was the last Washing defensive tackle to receive Pro Bowl recognition?

9. In 2016, which linebacker became the first Washington player to start all 16 games in each of his first six seasons in the NFL?

10. Colt McCoy threw a career long 71-yard touchdown pass to which receiver against Dallas in 2015?

11. 'Whiskey Red' was the nickname of which 1970s era quarterback?

12. What is the most wins the team has recorded in a single regular season?

13. What is the fewest number of wins the team has recorded in a single regular season?

14. Who are the two Washington quarterbacks to have won NFC Player of the Month honors?

15. Which member of the 2017 Hall of Fame class spent a single season with Washington in 2008?

16. Who had more 300-yard passing games for Washington – Jason Campbell or Doug Williams?

17. Which 2022 NFL head coach was a member of Washington's 1987 World Championship-winning team?

18. What number jersey did quarterback Kirk Cousins wear in his rookie season?

19. Up to the start of the 2022 season, how many regular season games had the team lost in franchise history? a) 602 b) 612 c) 622

20. Mark Moseley set the franchise record for the most points in a single season in 1983 with how many? a) 141 b) 151 c) 161

Quiz 13: Answers

1. George Allen 2. Miami 3. Miami 14-7 Washington 4. Billy Kilmer 5. Dallas 6. Mike Bass 7. Larry Brown, Mike Thomas and John Riggins 8. True 9. Minnesota 10. Chris Hanburger 11. Charley Taylor 12. Larry Brown 13. Jean Fugett 14. Jack Pardee 15. Billy Kilmer 16. Ken Houston 17. Lemar Parrish 18. Randy Johnson 19. c) 11 20. a) 8

Quiz 15: 1980s

1. Before being appointed the head coach of Washington, Joe Gibbs was the offensive coordinator of which team?

2. What was the only team to defeat Washington throughout the whole of the 1982 season?

3. Who returned an interception for a touchdown in the latter stages of the 1982 NFC Championship against the Cowboys to seal a famous win?

4. Which Washington player was named the NFL's MVP for 1982?

5. Which team routed Washington 38-9 in Super Bowl XVIII?

6. Which quarterback had a regular season starting record of 24-7 between 1985 and 1987?

7. Which alliteratively named defensive back led the NFL in interceptions in 1983 with nine?

8. True or false – Washington lost their first five games with Joe Gibbs as head coach?

9. Who were the four Washington players to lead the team in receiving yards in a season in the 1980s?

10. Washington was involved in the highest-scoring game in the history of Monday Night Football, losing 48-47 to which team in October 1983?

11. Washington routed which team 51-7 in a January 1984 playoff game?

12. Who were the three Washington quarterbacks to win 10 or more games in the 1980s?

13. True or false – In a 1980 game against the Cardinals, the dominant Washington defense gave up -12 passing yards?

14. Joe Theismann suffered a career-ending broken leg in a 1985 game against which team?

15. Who caught 11 passes for 241 yards but still ended up on the losing side in a 1986 game against the Giants?

16. Who returned a punt for a crucial 52-yard touchdown in a 1987 divisional round playoff game against the Bears?

17. Washington defeated which team in the NFC Championship game to reach Super Bowl XXII?

18. Which team defeated Washington 17-0 in the 1986 NFC Championship game?

19. How many losing seasons did Washington suffer during the 1980s? a) zero b) one c) two

20. What was the fewest number of games that Washington lost in a single season in the 1980s? a) one b) two c) three

Quiz 14: Answers

1. Winning 2. Ken Harvey 3. Mike Shanahan 4. Joe Jacoby 5. Bram Weinstein 6. True 7. Marv Levy 8. Dave Butz 9. Ryan Kerrigan 10. Rashad Ross 11. Billy Kilmer 12. 14 wins 13. 3 wins 14. Kirk Cousins and Todd Collins 15. Jason Taylor 16. Jason Campbell 17. Todd Bowles 18. #12 19. c) 622 games 20. c) 161 points

Quiz 16: Pot Luck

1. Does Washington have a better winning percentage in games played in December or January?

2. Does Washington have a winning or losing record in games against Dallas?

3. Which Washington running back was named the NFL's MVP in 1972?

4. How old was Jay Gruden when he was appointed Washington' head coach?

5. Which former tight end majored in art at college and has his own gallery?

6. Who holds the record for the most punt return touchdowns in franchise history with seven?

7. Which lineman sacked Aaron Rodgers for a safety in the 2015 Wild Card game against Green Bay?

8. Washington was routed 59-28 in a Monday Night Football game in 2010 against which division rival?

9. Which Washington safety went to seven straight Pro Bowls between 1973 and 1979?

10. Which Washington defender recorded 10 or more sacks every year from 1983 through to 1986?

11. Which trio of wide receivers was known collectively as 'The Posse'?

12. True or false – Running back John Riggins never went to the Pro Bowl while with Washington?

13. Which former Washington quarterback was the head coach at Grambling State University between 1998 and 2003 and again from 2011 to 2013?

14. What number jersey does quarterback Carson Wentz wear?

15. Which running back set a franchise record after rushing for eight touchdowns in his rookie year in 1998?

16. Who broke the NFL record for the most career catches by a running back during a brief spell in Washington in 2000?

17. The first ever game played by Washington was against which long-time rival?

18. Who is Washington's all-time leading point scorer in playoff games?

19. What was the average attendance at FedEx Field in 2021? a) 52,751 b) 62,751 c) 72,751

20. How many passes did Darrell Green intercept in his stellar career? a) 34 b) 44 c) 54

Quiz 15: Answers

1. San Diego 2. Dallas 3. Daryl Grant 4. Mark Moseley 5. L.A. Raiders 6. Jay Schroeder 7. Mark Murphy 8. True 9. Art Monk, Ricky Sanders, Gary Clark and Charlie Brown 10. Green Bay 11. L.A. Rams 12. Joe Theismann, Jay Schroeder and Mark Rypien 13. True 14. New York Giants 15. Gary Clark 16. Darrell Green 17. Minnesota 18. New York Giants 19. c) two 20. a) one.

Quiz 17: 1990s

1. Washington won how many consecutive games to start the 1991 season?

2. Washington recorded a franchise record 45-point win in the 1991 season opener against which team?

3. Washington routed which team in the NFC Championship game to reach Super Bowl XXVI?

4. Which long-time defensive coordinator succeeded Joe Gibbs as head coach in 1993?

5. Which wide receiver's 1,397 yards in 1993 are good enough for third spot on the team's most yards in a season list?

6. True or false – In a 1994 game against the Bucs Washington rushed for just 10 yards?

7. Which three Washington quarterbacks were voted to the Pro Bowl in the 1990s?

8. How many division titles did Washington win in the 1990s?

9. Washington racked up 56 points in a 1991 rout of which NFC rival?

10. In what year did Washington play their last game at RFK Stadium?

11. Which team did Washington face in that final game at RFK?

12. Washington started the 1998 season with how many straight losses?

13. Who was Washington's coach from 1994 through to the end of the decade?

14. Which alliteratively named punter went to the Pro Bowl in 1994?

15. Washington defeated which team 19-13 in overtime in the first regular season game played at FedEx Field?

16. Before Alfred Morris, you have to go back to 1993 to find the last rookie to lead the team in rushing. Who was that back?

17. Which Super Bowl-winning quarterback with the New York Giants won two of his three starts with Washington in 1997?

18. In 1999, two Washington receivers recorded 1,000-yard seasons. Which two?

19. How many regular season games did Washington win in their 1991 World Championship run? a) 12 b) 13 c) 14

20. In 1991 Washington offensive line gave up how many sacks? a) 9 b) 13 c) 17

Quiz 16: Answers

1. January 2. Losing 3. Larry Brown 4. 46 5. Chris Cooley 6. Brian Mitchell 7. Preston Smith 8. Philadelphia 9. Ken Houston 10. Dexter Manley 11. Art Monk, Gary Clark and Ricky Sanders 12. True 13. Doug Williams 14. #11 15. Skip Hicks 16. Larry Centers 17. New York Giants 18. John Riggins 19. a) 52,751 20. c) 54

Quiz 18: Pot Luck

1. Which member of 'The Hogs' was inducted into the Pro Football Hall of Fame in 2010?

2. Which diminutive receiver, who enjoyed five 1,000-yard seasons, joined Washington in 1985 after two years in the USFL with the Jacksonville Bulls?

3. Which former linebacker is a color commentator on Commanders' radio broadcasts?

4. True or false – Washington didn't have a first-round draft pick between 1984 and 1989?

5. Which member of the 'Hogs' was known to his teammates as 'Jake'?

6. Since 1970, three Washington head coaches have amassed 50 or more wins. George Allen and Joe Gibbs are two. Who is the third?

7. True or false – In a 1989 game against the Raiders Washington fumbled the ball eight times?

8. Whose 78-yard fumble return for a touchdown against the Colts in 1993 is the longest in franchise history?

9. Does Washington have a winning or losing record in Monday Night Football games?

10. Washington gave up 31 points in the fourth quarter of a 2013 game against which AFC West team?

11. The highlight of which wide receiver's Washington career was a 99-yard kickoff return touchdown against Carolina in 2015?

12. True or false – Washington has never played a playoff game that's gone to overtime?

13. Which Washington rookie caught six passes for 208 yards and a touchdown against the Panthers in October 2001?

14. Who had more 100-yard rushing games with Washington – Earnest Byner of Alfred Morris?

15. Who was the only Washington starter in Super Bowl XXVI whose full name started and ended with the same letter? (clue – he was a defensive back)

16. Since the 1970 merger, only two Washington first-round draft pick have a surname which ends in a vowel. Which two?

17. What number jersey did legendary wide receiver Art Monk wear?

18. Which left-handed Arizona quarterback set the record for the most passing yards in a single game against Washington in November 1996?

19. Which team has Washington beaten the most often in postseason games? a) Chicago b) Green Bay c) San Francisco

20. The 2012 team set the franchise record for the fewest turnovers in a season. How many times did they give up the ball? a) 12 b) 13 c) 14

Quiz 17: Answers

1. 11 games 2. Detroit 3. Detroit 4. Richie Petitbon 5. Henry Ellard 6. True 7. Mark Rypien, Brad Johnson and Gus Frerotte 8. Two 9. Atlanta 10. 1996 11. Dallas 12. Seven 13. Norv Turner 14. Reggie Roby 15. Arizona 16. Reggie Brooks 17. Jeff Hostetler 18. Michael Westbrook and Albert Connell 19. c) 14 games 20. a) Nine

Quiz 19: 2000s

1. Which former Browns and Chiefs head coach was appointed Washington's head coach in January 2001?

2. Which six-time Pro Bowl tackle did Washington select with the third overall pick of the 2000 NFL Draft?

3. In 2002, who became Washington's fifth new head coach in just 10 years?

4. Who were the three players to rush for over 1,000 yards in a season during the 2000s?

5. Which linebacker went to the Pro Bowl in 2001, 2002 and 2003?

6. Who was the only head coach to steer Washington to the playoffs in the 2000s?

7. Who were the three players to enjoy 1,000-yard receiving seasons in the 2000s?

8. Who led the team in interceptions for three straight years from 2001 through to 2003?

9. Which quarterback won nine of his 15 starts in 2005 to steer Washington to its first playoff berth since 1999?

10. Which kicker tied a franchise record after successfully converting five field goals against the Jets in November 2007?

11. Who were the two Washington defenders to record four sacks in a single game during the 2000s?

12. True or false – In 2006, Washington recorded just 19 sacks and 6 interceptions?

13. In 2003 Washington lost how many straight games?

14. Which former Seattle quarterback was the head coach in Washington in 2008 and 2009?

15. Which Washington tight end went to the Pro Bowl in both 2007 and 2008?

16. Who led the team in sacks every year from 2006 through to 2009?

17. Who were the only three Washington quarterbacks with more starting wins than losses in games played in the 2000s?

18. In 2009, who set the record for the most sacks by a Washington rookie with 11?

19. What was the highest number of wins recorded by Washington in a single season during the 2000s? a) 9 b) 10 c) 11

20. How many playoff games did Washington win throughout the decade? a) zero b) one c) two

Quiz 18: Answers

1. Russ Grimm 2. Gary Clark 3. London Fletcher 4. True 5. Joe Jacoby 6. Norv Turner 7. True 8. Darrell Green 9. Losing 10. Denver 11. Andre Roberts 12. True 13. Rod Gardner 14. Alfred Morris 15. Danny Copeland 16. Brian Orakpo and Daron Payne 17. #81 18. Boomer Esiason 19. a) Chicago 20. c) 14

Quiz 20: Pot Luck

1. Washington has recorded more wins over which opponent than any other?

2. Washington drafted Robert Griffin III from which college?

3. Who is the only Washington rookie to rush for 200 yards in a game?

4. Which former 'Hog' was the team's offensive line coach from 1992 to 2000?

5. By what name was Fedex Field formerly known?

6. Up to the start of the 2022 season and including playoff games, does Washington have an overall winning or losing record?

7. 'Slick Rick' was the nickname of which receiver who was with the team between 1986 and 1993?

8. Which former number one overall pick was 1-6 as a starter in Washington in 2000 and 2001?

9. Washington defeated which team in the 2005 Wild Card game?

10. Who was the first Washington quarterback to throw four touchdown passes in successive games?

11. True or false – Former running back John Riggins has appeared in the TV drama 'Law and Order: Criminal Intent'?

12. Who were the two offensive starters on Washington's Super Bowl XXII-winning team whose first name and surname started with the same letter?

13. Which female singer-songwriter sang the national anthem in the first ever game at FedEx Field?

14. Defensive great Dexter Manley wore what number jersey?

15. Which punter holds the record for the most kicks downed inside the 20-yard line in a season with 33?

16. Since 1982, who is the only Washington first-round draft pick whose first name and surname start with the same letter?

17. Which two Washington coaches from the 2000s had identical records of 12 wins and 20 losses?

18. In which round of the 2020 NFL Draft did Washington select running back Antonio Gibson?

19. Which opponent has scored the most touchdowns against Washington in franchise history? a) Tony Dorsett b) Michael Irvin c) Emmitt Smith

20. How many playoff games did Washington lose at RFK Stadium? a) one b) two c) three

Quiz 19: Answers

1. Marty Schottenheimer 2. Chris Samuels 3. Steve Spurrier 4. Clinton Portis, Ladell Betts, Stephen Davis 5. LaVar Arrington 6. Joe Gibbs 7. Rod Gardner, Laveranues Coles and Santana Moss 8. Fred Smoot 9. Mark Brunell 10. Shaun Suisham 11. Brian Orakpo and Phillip Daniels 12. True 13. Eight 14. Jim Zorn 15. Chris Cooley 16. Andre Carter 17. Brad Johnson, Tony Banks and Todd Collins 18. Brian Orakpo 19. b) 10 wins 20. b) one

Quiz 21: 2010 and Beyond

1. Which running back set a franchise record after catching 14 passes in a 2011 game against the 49ers?

2. Washington was involved in a blockbuster trade with which team that allowed them to draft Robert Griffin III?

3. The 2012 team suffered a 24-14 Wild Card round loss to which team?

4. How many games did Washington win in Ron Rivera's first season as head coach?

5. Which special teams ace went to the Pro Bowl in 2012?

6. Which quarterback had a record of five wins and eight losses in his only season in Washington in 2010?

7. True or false – Washington reached the playoffs in 2012 despite conceding more points than they scored?

8. Which Washington defender recorded four sacks in a 2014 game against Jacksonville?

9. Kirk Cousins won his first game as a starter in 2012 against which hapless AFC team?

10. True or false – Kirk Cousins led the team in rushing touchdowns in 2015?

11. Washington overturned a franchise record 24-point deficit in October 2015, eventually beating which NFC team 31-30?

12. In October 2016, Washington made its first regular season appearance in London. Which team did they face?

13. Who scored a hat-trick of rushing touchdowns in a 2016 game against Green Bay?

14. Who picked off four passes in a 2010 game against Chicago?

15. Kirk Cousins threw a 77-yard touchdown on his fourth pass attempt on his pro debut in 2012. Who caught it?

16. Washington played in front of their biggest ever road crowd in a 2016 game against which team?

17. Which defensive star appeared alongside Von Miller in an advert for the aftershave, Old Spice?

18. Between 2010 and 2021 only one Washington quarterback had a winning record as a starter. Which one?

19. Washington set an unwanted franchise record after giving up how many points in 2013? a) 458 b) 468 c) 478

20. How many games did Washington win in Mike Shanahan's final season as head coach? a) three b) four c) five

Quiz 20: Answers

1. Philadelphia 2. Baylor 3. Alfred Morris 4. Russ Grimm 5. Jack Kent Cooke Stadium 6. Losing 7. Ricky Sanders 8. Jeff George 9. Tampa Bay 10. Robert Griffin III 11. True 12. Joe Jacoby and Mark May 13. Mary Chapin Carpenter 14. #72 15. Matt Turk 16. LaRon Landry 17. Jim Zorn and Steve Spurrier 18. Third 19. c) Emmitt Smith 20. a) One

Quiz 22: Pot Luck

1. Washington has suffered more losses at the hands of which opponent than any other?

2. Which Washington star was known as 'Ageless Wonder'?

3. Who holds the franchise record for the most receiving yards in a season by a tight end?

4. True or false – Washington has never won on Thanksgiving Day?

5. Who holds the franchise record for the most seasons with 10 or more sacks?

6. Which legendary head coach spent a single season with Washington in 1969?

7. Which tackle went to the Pro Bowl six times between 2002 and 2008?

8. RFK Stadium was named after whom?

9. Who are the two Washington cornerbacks to start all 16 games in their rookie season?

10. Washington defeated which team 72-41 in a wild 1966 encounter?

11. In what year did Daniel Snyder assume ownership of Washington franchise?

12. Which running back won the NFL Offensive Rookie of the Year Award in 1975?

13. How old was Joe Gibbs when he was appointed Washington's head coach for the first time?

14. On which two days of the week has Washington never played a competitive game?

15. True or false – In the 1972 NFL Draft Washington didn't make their first pick until round eight?

16. Who rushed for a franchise record 90-yard touchdown in a December 2018 game?

17. That record long rushing touchdown was scored in a game against which opponent?

18. Who was the only Washington starter in Super Bowl XXII whose surname ended with a vowel?

19. Punter Tress Way set a franchise record in 2016 for the fewest punts in a full regular season. How many times did he kick? a) 49 b) 54 c) 59

20. Washington led the NFL in scoring in 1983 with how many points? a) 521 b) 531 c) 541

Quiz 21: Answers

1. Roy Helu Jr 2. St. Louis Rams 3. Seattle 4. Seven games 5. Lorenzo Alexander 6. Donovan McNabb 7. False 8. Ryan Kerrigan 9. Cleveland 10. True 11. Tampa Bay 12. Cincinnati 13. Rob Kelley 14. DeAngelo Hall 15. Santana Moss 16. Dallas 17. Montez Sweat 18. Alex Smith 19. c) 478 points 20. a) Three

Quiz 23: Numbers Game

What number jersey number did the following players wear?

1. Mark Rypien and DeSean Jackson

2. Doug Williams and Jason Campbell

3. Jamison Crowder and Laveranues Coles

4. Mark Moseley and Dustin Hopkins

5. Josh Norman and Champ Bailey

6. Alfred Morris and LaDell Betts

7. Brad Dusek and London Fletcher

8. Terry Allen and Earnest Byner

9. Gary Clark and Niles Paul

10. Charles Mann and Trent Williams

11. Clinton Portis and Bashaud Breeland

12. Brian Mitchell and LaRon Landry

13. Raleigh McKenzie and Will Montgomery

14. Chip Lohmiller and Mark Brunell

15. Robert Griffin III and Trent Green

16. Bruce Smith and Kory Lichtensteiger

17. Clint Didier and Jordan Reed

18. Tress Way and Heath Shuler

19. Gus Frerotte and Tony Banks

20. Don Warren and Vernon Davis

Quiz 22: Answers

1. New York Giants 2. Darrell Green 3. Jordan Reed 4. False 5. Charles Mann 6. Vince Lombardi 7. Chris Samuels 8. Robert F. Kennedy 9. Darrell Green and Champ Bailey 10. New York Giants 11. 1999 12. Mike Thomas 13. 40 years old 14. Wednesday and Friday 15. True 16. Adrian Peterson 17. Philadelphia 18. Raleigh McKenzie 19. a) 49 times 20. c) 541

Quiz 24: Pot Luck

1. Who holds the franchise record for the most career interception-return touchdowns?

2. Which player authored the 2013 book, 'Game Changer: Faith, Football, & Finding Your Way'?

3. Which tight end started his 150th NFL game against the Cardinals in December 2016?

4. In 2021, who became the first Washington inside linebacker since London Fletcher to return an interception for a touchdown?

5. Whose 31-yard pass to Quinton Dunbar against the Giants in September 2016 was his first career completion?

6. Who are the three Washington quarterbacks to pass for 3,000 yards and rush for 300 yards in the same season?

7. Whose number 21 jersey number was retired in October 2021?

8. The Commanders franchise started life in which city?

9. Before moving to RFK Stadium, where did Washington call home?

10. Washington has won more games in which month than any other?

11. Who are the three Washington head coaches to have been named the Associated Press NFL Coach of the Year?

12. In November 1986, Washington raced into a record-breaking 34-0 half-time lead against which divisional rival?

13. Which defensive lineman returned an Andy Dalton pick to score his first career touchdown in a November 2020 game against Dallas?

14. Did the team have a winning or losing overall record at RFK Stadium?

15. Who caught a 40-yard touchdown pass from Gus Frerotte to secure an overtime victory for Washington in the first game played at FedEx Field?

16. Who was the only Washington starter in Super Bowl XXII whose surname started with a vowel? (clue – it was a linebacker)

17. True or false – Darrell Green was a member of the 1984 US Olympic 4x100m relay team?

18. Which starting quarterback won more games while with Washington – Brad Johnson or Robert Griffin III?

19. Which of these three quarterbacks threw the most touchdown passes while with Washington? a) Mark Brunell b) Gus Frerotte c) Jason Campbell

20. What is Washington's highest average attendance over a full season? a) 85,625 b) 87,625 c) 89,625

Quiz 23: Answers

1. #11 2. #17 3. #80 4. #3 5. #24 6. #46 7. #59 8. #21 9. #84 10. #71 11. #26 12. #30 13. #63 14. #8 15. #10 16. #72 17. #86 18. #5 19. #12 20. #85

Quiz 25: Anagrams

1. I Beg Jobs

2. Not Mark

3. Kick Our Sins

4. Near Gray Ink

5. Ringing Josh

6. Larger Lender

7. Coin Sprint Lot

8. Dare Meet Lynx

9. Amass No Ants

10. French Lend Loot

11. Ordered Jan

12. Memory Leaks

13. He Not Jasmine

14. Maul Idols Wig

15. Into Onion Bags

16. Tin Watermills

17. A Merry Pink

18. Ramrod Rifles

19. Rams Channel

20. Trimly Run Race

Quiz 24: Answers

1. Darrell Green 2. Kirk Cousins 3. Vernon Davis 4. Cole Holcomb 5. Tress Way 6. Robert Griffin III, Joe Theismann and Taylor Heinicke 7. Sean Taylor 8. Boston 9. Griffith Stadium 10. October 11. George Allen, Jack Pardee and Joe Gibbs 12. Dallas 13. Montez Sweat 14. Winning 15. Michael Westbrook 16. Neal Olkewicz 17. False 18. Brad Johnson 19. c) Jason Campbell 20. c) 89,625

www.ingramcontent.com/pod-product-compliance
Lightning Source LLC
Chambersburg PA
CBHW071506070426
42452CB00041B/2441